30 Scripture Readings on Forgiveness

Year Long Bible Reading Series

Edited by James David Rae

TheBiblePeople.com

30 Scripture Readings on Forgiveness
© TheBiblePeople.com
Edited by James David Rae

Scripture quotations marked NIV are taken from the HOLY BIBLE, NEW INTERNATIONAL VERSION Copyright © 1973, 1978, 1984 by International Bible Society. Used by permission of Zondervan Publishing House. All rights reserved.

Scripture quotations marked NLT are taken from the HOLY BIBLE, NEW LIVING TRANSLATION copyright © 1996. Used by permission of Tyndale House Publishers, Inc., Wheaton, Illinois 60189. All rights reserved.

Scripture quotations marked NRSV are taken from the NEW REVISED STANDARD VERSION BIBLE, copyright 1989, Division of Christian Education of the National Council of the Churches of Christ in the United States of America. Used by permission. All rights reserved.

Scripture quotations marked ESV are taken from The Holy Bible: English Standard Version, copyright © 2001, Wheaton: Good News Publishers. Used by permission. All rights reserved.

Scripture quotations marked GWT are taken from the God's Word® Translation. Copyright © 1995 by God's Word to the Nations. Published by Baker Book House. Used by permission.

Introduction

As Christians, one of the most difficult opportunities we face is to forgive those who hurt us. If Jesus was able to forgive the soldiers who crucified Him, why do we find it so hard to forgive the people who hurt us? Pain, regret and bitterness should not be the center of a Christian's life, rather we should be responsive and generous to those who hurt us and then seek forgiveness.

Forgiveness for us is not a choice, but a command. Through these30 daily scripture readings, you'll find examples of forgiveness and read passages about God's great forgiveness for us.

Invest a few minutes each day with this book. You'll find that after a month, you begin to feel the freedom that forgiveness brings, and a deep, residing joy despite a painful past.

These 30 passages are reprinted in their entirety but without commentary in hopes that you will enjoy reflective, undistracted moments with God's Word.

Reading 1: A Brother Forgives

Genesis 32:1-21; 33:1-11

Jacob also went on his way, and the angels of God met him. When Jacob saw them, he said, "This is the camp of God!" So he named that place Mahanaim.

Jacob sent messengers ahead of him to his brother Esau in the land of Seir, the country of Edom. He instructed them: "This is what you are to say to my master Esau: 'Your servant Jacob says, I have been staying with Laban and have remained there till now. I have cattle and donkeys, sheep and goats, menservants and maidservants. Now I am sending this message to my lord, that I may find favor in your eyes.' "

When the messengers returned to Jacob, they said, "We went to your brother Esau, and now he is coming to meet you, and four hundred men are with him."

In great fear and distress Jacob divided the people who were with him into two groups, and the flocks and herds and camels as well. He thought, "If Esau comes and attacks one group, the group that is left may escape."

Then Jacob prayed, "O God of my father Abraham, God of my father Isaac, O Lord, who said to me, 'Go back to your country and your relatives, and I will make you prosper,' I am unworthy of all the kindness and faithfulness you have shown your servant. I had only my staff when I crossed this Jordan, but now I have become two groups. Save me, I pray, from the hand of my brother Esau, for I am afraid he will come and attack me, and also the mothers with their children.

But you have said, 'I will surely make you prosper and will make your descendants like the sand of the sea, which cannot be counted.' "

He spent the night there, and from what he had with him he selected a gift for his brother Esau: two hundred female goats and twenty male goats, two hundred ewes and twenty rams, thirty female camels with their young, forty cows and ten bulls, and twenty female donkeys and ten male donkeys. He put them in the care of his servants, each herd by itself, and said to his servants, "Go ahead of me, and keep some space between the herds."

He instructed the one in the lead: "When my brother Esau meets you and asks, 'To whom do you belong, and where are you going, and who owns all these animals in front of you?' then you are to say, 'They belong to your servant Jacob. They are a gift sent to my lord Esau, and he is coming behind us.' "

He also instructed the second, the third and all the others who followed the herds: "You are to say the same thing to Esau when you meet him. And be sure to say, 'Your servant Jacob is coming behind us.' " For he thought, "I will pacify him with these gifts I am sending on ahead; later, when I see him, perhaps he will receive me." So Jacob's gifts went on ahead of him, but he himself spent the night in the camp.

Jacob looked up and there was Esau, coming with his four hundred men; so he divided the children among Leah, Rachel and the two maidservants. He put the maidservants and their children in front, Leah and her children next, and Rachel and Joseph in the rear. He himself went on ahead and bowed down to the ground seven times as he approached his brother.

But Esau ran to meet Jacob and embraced him; he threw his arms around his neck and kissed him. And they wept. Then Esau looked up and saw the women and children. "Who are these with you?" he asked.

Jacob answered, "They are the children God has graciously given your servant."

Then the maidservants and their children approached and bowed down. Next, Leah and her children came and bowed down. Last of all came Joseph and Rachel, and they too bowed down.

Esau asked, "What do you mean by all these droves I met?"

"To find favor in your eyes, my lord," he said.

But Esau said, "I already have plenty, my brother. Keep what you have for yourself."

"No, please!" said Jacob. "If I have found favor in your eyes, accept this gift from me. For to see your face is like seeing the face of God, now that you have received me favorably. Please accept the present that was brought to you, for God has been gracious to me and I have all I need." And because Jacob insisted, Esau accepted it. (NIV)

Reading 2: The Transgression of Your Brothers

Genesis 50:1-21

Then Joseph threw himself on his father's face and wept over him and kissed him. Joseph commanded the physicians in his service to embalm his father. So the physicians embalmed Israel; they spent forty days in doing this, for that is the time required for embalming. And the Egyptians wept for him seventy days.

When the days of weeping for him were past, Joseph addressed the household of Pharaoh, "If now I have found favor with you, please speak to Pharaoh as follows: My father made me swear an oath; he said, 'I am about to die. In the tomb that I hewed out for myself in the land of Canaan, there you shall bury me.' Now therefore let me go up, so that I may bury my father; then I will return." Pharaoh answered, "Go up, and bury your father, as he made you swear to do."

So Joseph went up to bury his father. With him went up all the servants of Pharaoh, the elders of his household, and all the elders of the land of Egypt, as well as all the household of Joseph, his brothers, and his father's household. Only their children, their flocks, and their herds were left in the land of Goshen. Both chariots and charioteers went up with him. It was a very great company. When they came to the threshing floor of Atad, which is beyond the Jordan, they held there a very great and sorrowful lamentation; and he observed a time of mourning for his father seven days. When the Canaanite inhabitants of the land saw the mourning on the threshing floor of Atad, they said, "This is a grievous mourning on the part of the Egyptians." Therefore the place was named Abel-mizraim; it is beyond the Jordan. Thus his sons did for him as he had instructed them. They carried him to the land of Canaan and buried him in the cave of the field at Machpelah, the field near Mamre, which Abraham bought as a burial site from Ephron the Hittite. After he had buried his father, Joseph returned to Egypt with his brothers and all who had gone up with him to bury his father.

Realizing that their father was dead, Joseph's brothers said, "What if Joseph still bears a grudge against us and pays us back in full for all the wrong that we did to him?" So they approached Joseph, saying, "Your father gave this instruction before he died, 'Say to Joseph: I beg you, forgive the crime of your brothers and the wrong they did in harming you.' Now therefore please forgive the crime of the servants of the God of your father." Joseph wept when they spoke to him. Then his brothers also wept, fell down before him, and said, "We are here as your slaves." But Joseph said to them, "Do not be afraid! Am I in the place of God? Even though you intended to do harm to me, God intended it for good, in order to preserve a numerous people, as he is doing today. So have no fear; I myself will provide for you and your little ones." In this way he reassured them, speaking kindly to them. (NRSV)

Reading 3: A God Merciful and Gracious

Exodus 34:1-35

The Lord told Moses, "Prepare two stone tablets like the first ones. I will write on them the same words that were on the tablets you smashed. Be ready in the morning to come up Mount Sinai and present yourself to me there on the top of the mountain. No one else may come with you. In fact, no one is allowed anywhere on the mountain. Do not even let the flocks or herds graze near the mountain."

So Moses cut two tablets of stone like the first ones. Early in the morning he climbed Mount Sinai as the Lord had told him, carrying the two stone tablets in his hands.

Then the Lord came down in a pillar of cloud and called out his own name, "the Lord," as Moses stood there in his presence. He passed in front of Moses and said, "I am the Lord, I am the Lord, the merciful and gracious God. I am slow to anger and rich in unfailing love and faithfulness. I show this unfailing love to many thousands by forgiving every kind of sin and rebellion. Even so I do not leave sin unpunished, but I punish the children for the sins of their parents to the third and fourth generations."

Moses immediately fell to the ground and worshiped. And he said, "If it is true that I have found favor in your sight, O Lord, then please go with us. Yes, this is an unruly and stubborn people, but please pardon our iniquity and our sins. Accept us as your own special possession."

The Lord replied, "All right. This is the covenant I am going to make with you. I will perform wonders that have never been done before anywhere in all the earth or in any nation. And all the people around you will see the power of the Lord—the awesome power I will display through you. Your responsibility is to obey all the commands I am giving you today. Then I will surely drive out all those who stand in your way—the Amorites, Canaanites, Hittites, Perizzites, Hivites, and Jebusites.

"Be very careful never to make treaties with the people in the land where you are going. If you do, you soon will be following their evil ways. Instead, you must break down their pagan altars, smash the sacred pillars they worship, and cut down their carved images. You must worship no other gods, but only the Lord, for he is a God who is passionate about his relationship with you.

"Do not make treaties of any kind with the people living in the land. They are spiritual prostitutes, committing adultery against me by sacrificing to their gods. If you make peace with them, they will invite you to go with them to worship their gods, and you are likely to do it. And you will accept their daughters, who worship other gods, as wives for your sons. Then they will cause your sons to commit adultery against me by worshiping other gods. You must make no gods for yourselves at all.

"Be sure to celebrate the Festival of Unleavened Bread for seven days, just as I instructed you, at the appointed time each year in early spring, for that was when you left Egypt.

"Every firstborn male belongs to me—of both cattle and sheep. A firstborn male donkey may be redeemed from the Lord by presenting a lamb in its place. But if you decide not to make the exchange, you must kill the donkey by breaking its neck. However, you must redeem every firstborn son. No one is allowed to appear before me without a gift.

"Six days are set aside for work, but on the Sabbath day you must rest, even during the seasons of plowing and harvest. And you must remember to celebrate the Festival of Harvest with the first crop of the wheat harvest, and celebrate the Festival of the Final Harvest at the end of the harvest season. Three times each year all the men of Israel must appear before the Sovereign Lord, the God of Israel. No one will attack and conquer your land when you go to appear before the Lord your God those three times each year. I will drive out the nations that stand in your way and will enlarge your boundaries.

"You must not offer bread made with yeast as a sacrifice to me. And none of the meat of the Passover lamb may be kept over until the following morning. You must bring the best of the first of each year's crop to the house of the Lord your God.

"You must not cook a young goat in its mother's milk."

And the Lord said to Moses, "Write down all these instructions, for they represent the terms of my covenant with you and with Israel."

Moses was up on the mountain with the Lord forty days and forty nights. In all that time he neither ate nor drank. At that time he wrote the terms of the covenant—the Ten Commandments—on the stone tablets.

When Moses came down the mountain carrying the stone tablets inscribed with the terms of the covenant, he wasn't aware that his face glowed because he had spoken to the Lord face to face. And when Aaron and the people of Israel saw the radiance of Moses' face, they were afraid to come near him.

But Moses called to them and asked Aaron and the community leaders to come over and talk with him. Then all the people came, and

Moses gave them the instructions the Lord had given him on Mount Sinai. When Moses had finished speaking with them, he put a veil over his face. But whenever he went into the Tent of Meeting to speak with the Lord, he removed the veil until he came out again. Then he would give the people whatever instructions the Lord had given him, and the people would see his face aglow. Afterward he would put the veil on again until he returned to speak with the Lord. (NLT)

Reading 4: No God Like You

I Kings 8:22-53

In the presence of the entire assembly of Israel, Solomon stood in front of the Lord's altar. He stretched out his hands toward heaven and said,

"Lord God of Israel,
 there is no god like you in heaven above or on earth below.
 You keep your promise of mercy to your servants,
  who obey you wholeheartedly.
 You have kept your promise to my father David, your servant.
  With your mouth you promised it.
  With your hand you carried it out as it is today.

"Now, Lord God of Israel,
 keep your promise to my father David, your servant.
 You said, 'You will never fail to have an heir
  sitting in front of me on the throne of Israel
  if your descendants are faithful to me
   as you have been faithful to me.'

"So now, God of Israel,
 may the promise you made to my father David,
 your servant, come true.

"Does God really live on earth?
If heaven itself, the highest heaven, cannot hold you,
then how can this temple that I have built?
Nevertheless, my Lord God, please pay attention to my prayer for mercy.
Listen to my cry for help as I pray to you today.
Night and day may your eyes be on this temple,
the place about which you said, 'My name will be there.'
Listen to me as I pray toward this place.
Hear the plea for mercy
that your people Israel and I pray toward this place.
Hear us {when we pray} to heaven, the place where you live.
Hear and forgive.

"If anyone sins against another person
and is required to take an oath
and comes to take the oath in front of your altar in this temple,
then hear {that person} in heaven, take action, and make a decision.
Condemn the guilty person with the proper punishment,
but declare the innocent person innocent.

"An enemy may defeat your people Israel
because they have sinned against you.
But when your people turn to you, praise your name, pray,
and plead with you in this temple,
then hear {them} in heaven, forgive the sins of your people Israel,
and bring them back to the land that you gave to their ancestors.

"When the sky is shut and there's no rain
 because they are sinning against you,
 and they pray toward this place, praise your name,
 and turn away from their sin because you made them suffer,
then hear {them} in heaven.
 Forgive the sins of your servants, your people Israel.
 Teach them the proper way to live.
 Then send rain on the land,
 which you gave to your people as an inheritance.

"There may be famine in the land.
Plant diseases, heat waves, funguses, locusts,
 or grasshoppers may destroy crops.
Enemies may blockade Israel's city gates.
During every plague or sickness
 {hear} every prayer for mercy,
 made by one person or by all the people in Israel,
 whose consciences bother them,
 who stretch out their hands toward this temple.
Hear {them} in heaven, where you live.
 Forgive {them}, and take action.
 Give each person the proper reply.
 (You know what is in their hearts,
 because you alone know what is in the hearts of all people.)
Then, as long as they live in the land that you gave to our ancestors,
 they will fear you.

"People will hear about your great name,
 mighty hand, and powerful arm.

So when people who are not Israelites
come from distant countries because of your name
to pray facing this temple,
hear {them} in heaven, the place where you live.
Do everything they ask you
so that all the people of the world may know your name
and fear you like your people Israel
and learn also that this temple which I built bears your name.

"When your people go to war against their enemies
(wherever you may send them)
and they pray to you, O Lord, toward the city you have chosen
and the temple I built for your name,
then hear their prayer for mercy in heaven,
and do what is right {for them}.

"They may sin against you.
(No one is sinless.)
You may become angry with them and hand them over to an enemy
who takes them to {another} country as captives,
{whether it is} far or near.
If they come to their senses,
are sorry for what they've done,
and plead with you in the land where they are captives,
saying, 'We have sinned. We have done wrong.
We have been wicked,'
if they change their attitude toward you
in the land of their enemies where they are captives,

if they pray to you
　　　toward the land that you gave their ancestors,
　　　and the city you have chosen,
　　　and the temple I have built for your name,
　　then in heaven, the place where you live, hear their prayer for mercy.
　　　Do what is right for them.
　　　Forgive your people, who have sinned against you.
　　　{Forgive} all their wrongs when they rebelled against you,
　　　　and cause those who captured them to have mercy on them
　　　　because they are your own people
　　　　whom you brought out of Egypt
　　　　from the middle of an iron smelter.

　　"May your eyes always see my plea and your people Israel's plea
　　　so that you will listen to them whenever they call on you.
　　After all, you, Lord God, set them apart from all the people of the world
　　　to be your own as you promised through your servant Moses
　　　when you brought our ancestors out of Egypt." (GWT)

Reading 5: May the Lord Pardon Everyone!

2 Chronicles 30:1-20

Hezekiah sent to all Israel and Judah, and wrote letters also to Ephraim and Manasseh, that they should come to the house of the Lord at Jerusalem to keep the Passover to the Lord, the God of Israel. For the king and his princes and all the assembly in Jerusalem had taken counsel to keep the Passover in the second month— for they could not keep it at that time because the priests had not consecrated themselves in sufficient number, nor had the people assembled in Jerusalem— and the plan seemed right to the king and all the assembly. So they decreed to make a proclamation throughout all Israel, from Beer-sheba to Dan, that the people should come and keep the Passover to the Lord, the God of Israel, at Jerusalem, for they had not kept it as often as prescribed. So couriers went throughout all Israel and Judah with letters from the king and his princes, as the king had commanded, saying, "O people of Israel, return to the Lord, the God of Abraham, Isaac, and Israel, that he may turn again to the remnant of you who have escaped from the hand of the kings of Assyria. Do not be like your fathers and your brothers, who were faithless to the Lord God of their fathers, so that he made them a desolation, as you see. Do not now be stiff-necked as your fathers were, but yield yourselves to the Lord and come to his sanctuary, which he has consecrated forever, and serve the Lord your God, that his fierce anger may turn away from you. For if you return to the Lord, your brothers and your children will find compassion with their captors and return to this land. For the Lord your God is gracious and merciful and will not turn away his face from you, if you return to him."

So the couriers went from city to city through the country of Ephraim and Manasseh, and as far as Zebulun, but they laughed them to scorn and mocked them. However, some men of Asher, of Manasseh, and of Zebulun humbled themselves and came to Jerusalem. The hand of God was also on Judah to give them one heart to do what the king and the princes commanded by the word of the Lord.

And many people came together in Jerusalem to keep the Feast of Unleavened Bread in the second month, a very great assembly. They set to work and removed the altars that were in Jerusalem, and all the altars for burning incense they took away and threw into the Kidron valley. And they slaughtered the Passover lamb on the fourteenth day of the second month. And the priests and the Levites were ashamed, so that they consecrated themselves and brought burnt offerings into the house of the Lord. They took their accustomed posts according to the Law of Moses the man of God. The priests threw the blood that they received from the hand of the Levites. For there were many in the assembly who had not consecrated themselves. Therefore the Levites had to slaughter the Passover lamb for everyone who was not clean, to consecrate it to the Lord. For a majority of the people, many of them from Ephraim, Manasseh, Issachar, and Zebulun, had not cleansed themselves, yet they ate the Passover otherwise than as prescribed. For Hezekiah had prayed for them, saying, "May the good Lord pardon everyone

who sets his heart to seek God, the Lord, the God of his fathers, even though not according to the sanctuary's rules of cleanness." And the Lord heard Hezekiah and healed the people. (ESV)

Reading 6: Remember Your Mercy, O Lord

Psalm 25:1-22

To you, O Lord, I lift up my soul;
in you I trust, O my God.
Do not let me be put to shame,
nor let my enemies triumph over me.
No one whose hope is in you
will ever be put to shame,
but they will be put to shame
who are treacherous without excuse.

Show me your ways, O Lord,
teach me your paths;
guide me in your truth and teach me,
for you are God my Savior,
and my hope is in you all day long.
Remember, O Lord, your great mercy and love,
for they are from of old.
Remember not the sins of my youth
and my rebellious ways;
according to your love remember me,
for you are good, O Lord.

Good and upright is the Lord;
therefore he instructs sinners in his ways.
He guides the humble in what is right
and teaches them his way.
All the ways of the Lord are loving and faithful
for those who keep the demands of his covenant.
For the sake of your name, O Lord,
forgive my iniquity, though it is great.
Who, then, is the man that fears the Lord?
He will instruct him in the way chosen for him.
He will spend his days in prosperity,
and his descendants will inherit the land.
The Lord confides in those who fear him;
he makes his covenant known to them.
My eyes are ever on the Lord,
for only he will release my feet from the snare.
Turn to me and be gracious to me,
for I am lonely and afflicted.
The troubles of my heart have multiplied;
free me from my anguish.
Look upon my affliction and my distress
and take away all my sins.
See how my enemies have increased and
how fiercely they hate me!
Guard my life and rescue me;
let me not be put to shame,

for I take refuge in you.
May integrity and uprightness protect me,
because my hope is in you.

Redeem Israel, O God,
from all their troubles! (NIV)

Reading 7: Blessed Are the Forgiven

Psalm 32:1-11

Happy are those whose transgression is forgiven,
whose sin is covered.
Happy are those to whom the Lord imputes no iniquity,
and in whose spirit there is no deceit.

While I kept silence, my body wasted away
through my groaning all day long.
For day and night your hand was heavy upon me;
my strength was dried up as by the heat of summer.
Selah

Then I acknowledged my sin to you,
and I did not hide my iniquity;
I said, "I will confess my transgressions to the Lord,"
and you forgave the guilt of my sin.
Selah

Therefore let all who are faithful
offer prayer to you;
at a time of distress, the rush of mighty waters
shall not reach them.
You are a hiding place for me;

you preserve me from trouble;
you surround me with glad cries of deliverance.
Selah

I will instruct you and teach you the way you should go;
I will counsel you with my eye upon you.
Do not be like a horse or a mule, without understanding,
whose temper must be curbed with bit and bridle,
else it will not stay near you.

Many are the torments of the wicked,
but steadfast love surrounds those who trust in the Lord.
Be glad in the Lord and rejoice, O righteous,
and shout for joy, all you upright in heart. (NRSV)

Reading 8: Show Us Your Steadfast Love

Psalm 85:1-12

For the choir director: A psalm of the descendants of Korah.

Lord, you have poured out amazing blessings on your land!
 You have restored the fortunes of Israel.
You have forgiven the guilt of your people—
 yes, you have covered all their sins.
Interlude

You have withdrawn your fury.
 You have ended your blazing anger.
Now turn to us again, O God of our salvation.
 Put aside your anger against us.
Will you be angry with us always?
 Will you prolong your wrath to distant generations?
Won't you revive us again,
 so your people can rejoice in you?
Show us your unfailing love, O Lord,
 and grant us your salvation.

I listen carefully to what God the Lord is saying,
 for he speaks peace to his people, his faithful ones.
But let them not return to their foolish ways.

Surely his salvation is near to those who honor him;
 our land will be filled with his glory.

Unfailing love and truth have met together.
 Righteousness and peace have kissed!
Truth springs up from the earth,
 and righteousness smiles down from heaven.
Yes, the Lord pours down his blessings.
 Our land will yield its bountiful crops. (NLT)

Reading 9: God Freely Pardons

Isaiah 55:1-13

"Listen! Whoever is thirsty, come to the water!
Whoever has no money can come, buy, and eat!
 Come, buy wine and milk. You don't have to pay; its free!
Why do you spend money on what cannot nourish you
 and your wages on what does not satisfy you?
Listen carefully to me:
 Eat what is good, and enjoy the best foods.
Open your ears, and come to me!
Listen so that you may live!
I will make an everlasting promise to you—
 the blessings I promised to David.
I made him a witness to people,
 a leader and a commander for people.
You will summon a nation that you don't know,
 and a nation that doesn't know you will run to you
 because of the Lord your God,
 because of the Holy One of Israel.
 He has honored you."

Seek the Lord while he may be found.
Call on him while he is near.
Let wicked people abandon their ways.
Let evil people abandon their thoughts.

Let them return to the Lord,
 and he will show compassion to them.
Let them return to our God,
 because he will freely forgive them.

"My thoughts are not your thoughts,
 and my ways are not your ways," declares the Lord.
"Just as the heavens are higher than the earth,
 so my ways are higher than your ways,
 and my thoughts are higher than your thoughts."

"Rain and snow come down from the sky.
 They do not go back again until they water the earth.
 They make it sprout and grow
  so that it produces seed for farmers
  and food for people to eat.
My word, which comes from my mouth, is like the rain and snow.
 It will not come back to me without results.
 It will accomplish whatever I want
 and achieve whatever I send it to do."

You will go out with joy and be led out in peace.
 The mountains and the hills
 will break into songs of joy in your presence,
  and all the trees will clap their hands.
Cypress trees will grow where thornbushes grew.
Myrtle trees will grow where briars grew.
 This will be a reminder of the Lord's name
 and an everlasting sign that will never be destroyed.
Isaiah 55:1-13 (GWT)

Reading 10: He Delights in Steadfast Love

Micah 7:1-20

Woe is me! For I have become as when the summer fruit has been gathered,
   as when the grapes have been gleaned:
there is no cluster to eat,
   no first-ripe fig that my soul desires.
The godly has perished from the earth,
   and there is no one upright among mankind;
they all lie in wait for blood,
   and each hunts the other with a net.
Their hands are on what is evil, to do it well;
   the prince and the judge ask for a bribe,
and the great man utters the evil desire of his soul;
   thus they weave it together.
The best of them is like a brier,
   the most upright of them a thorn hedge.
The day of your watchmen, of your punishment, has come;
   now their confusion is at hand.
Put no trust in a neighbor;
   have no confidence in a friend;
guard the doors of your mouth
   from her who lies in your arms;
for the son treats the father with contempt,

the daughter rises up against her mother,
the daughter-in-law against her mother-in-law;
a man's enemies are the men of his own house.
But as for me, I will look to the Lord;
I will wait for the God of my salvation;
my God will hear me.
Rejoice not over me, O my enemy;
when I fall, I shall rise;
when I sit in darkness,
the Lord will be a light to me.
I will bear the indignation of the Lord
because I have sinned against him,
until he pleads my cause
and executes judgment for me.
He will bring me out to the light;
I shall look upon his vindication.
Then my enemy will see,
and shame will cover her who said to me,
"Where is the Lord your God?"
My eyes will look upon her;
now she will be trampled down
like the mire of the streets.
A day for the building of your walls!
In that day the boundary shall be far extended.
In that day they will come to you,
from Assyria and the cities of Egypt,
and from Egypt to the River,

from sea to sea and from mountain to mountain.
But the earth will be desolate
 because of its inhabitants,
 for the fruit of their deeds.
Shepherd your people with your staff,
 the flock of your inheritance,
who dwell alone in a forest
 in the midst of a garden land;
let them graze in Bashan and Gilead
 as in the days of old.
As in the days when you came out of the land of Egypt,
 I will show them marvelous things.
The nations shall see and be ashamed of all their might;
they shall lay their hands on their mouths;
 their ears shall be deaf;
they shall lick the dust like a serpent,
 like the crawling things of the earth;
they shall come trembling out of their strongholds;
 they shall turn in dread to the Lord our God,
 and they shall be in fear of you.
Who is a God like you, pardoning iniquity
 and passing over transgression
 for the remnant of his inheritance?
He does not retain his anger forever,
 because he delights in steadfast love.
He will again have compassion on us;
 he will tread our iniquities under foot.

You will cast all our sins
 into the depths of the sea.
You will show faithfulness to Jacob
 and steadfast love to Abraham,
as you have sworn to our fathers
 from the days of old. (ESV)

Reading 11: Forgive Us Our Debts

Matthew 6:5-15

"And when you pray, do not be like the hypocrites, for they love to pray standing in the synagogues and on the street corners to be seen by men. I tell you the truth, they have received their reward in full. But when you pray, go into your room, close the door and pray to your Father, who is unseen. Then your Father, who sees what is done in secret, will reward you. And when you pray, do not keep on babbling like pagans, for they think they will be heard because of their many words. Do not be like them, for your Father knows what you need before you ask him.

"This, then, is how you should pray:

" 'Our Father in heaven,
hallowed be your name,
your kingdom come,
your will be done
on earth as it is in heaven.
Give us today our daily bread.
Forgive us our debts,
as we also have forgiven our debtors.
And lead us not into temptation,
but deliver us from the evil one.'

For if you forgive men when they sin against you, your heavenly Father will also forgive you. But if you do not forgive men their sins, your Father will not forgive your sins. (NIV)

Reading 12: Parable of the Unforgiving Servant

Matthew 18:15-35

"If another member of the church sins against you, go and point out the fault when the two of you are alone. If the member listens to you, you have regained that one. But if you are not listened to, take one or two others along with you, so that every word may be confirmed by the evidence of two or three witnesses. If the member refuses to listen to them, tell it to the church; and if the offender refuses to listen even to the church, let such a one be to you as a Gentile and a tax collector. Truly I tell you, whatever you bind on earth will be bound in heaven, and whatever you loose on earth will be loosed in heaven. Again, truly I tell you, if two of you agree on earth about anything you ask, it will be done for you by my Father in heaven. For where two or three are gathered in my name, I am there among them."

Then Peter came and said to him, "Lord, if another member of the church sins against me, how often should I forgive? As many as seven times?" Jesus said to him, "Not seven times, but, I tell you, seventy-seven times.

"For this reason the kingdom of heaven may be compared to a king who wished to settle accounts with his slaves. When he began the reckoning, one who owed him ten thousand talents was brought to him; and, as he could not pay, his lord ordered him to be sold, together with his wife and children and all his possessions, and payment to be made. So the slave fell on his knees before him, saying, 'Have patience with me, and I will pay you everything.' And out of pity for him, the lord of that slave released him and forgave him the debt. But that same slave, as he went out, came upon one of his fellow slaves who owed him a hundred denarii; and seizing him by the throat, he said, 'Pay what you owe.' Then his fellow slave fell down and pleaded with him, 'Have patience with me, and I will pay you.' But he refused; then he went and threw him into prison until he would pay the debt. When his fellow slaves saw what had happened, they were greatly distressed, and they went and reported to their lord all that had taken place. Then his lord summoned him and said to him, 'You wicked slave! I forgave you all that debt because you pleaded with me. Should you not have had mercy on your fellow slave, as I had mercy on you?' And in anger his lord handed him over to be tortured until he would pay his entire debt. So my heavenly Father will also do to every one of you, if you do not forgive your brother or sister from your heart." (NRSV)

Reading 13: Poured Out for Forgiveness

Matthew 26:17-29

On the first day of the Festival of Unleavened Bread, the disciples came to Jesus and asked, "Where do you want us to prepare the Passover supper?"

"As you go into the city," he told them, "you will see a certain man. Tell him, 'The Teacher says, My time has come, and I will eat the Passover meal with my disciples at your house.' " So the disciples did as Jesus told them and prepared the Passover supper there.

When it was evening, Jesus sat down at the table with the twelve disciples. While they were eating, he said, "The truth is, one of you will betray me."

Greatly distressed, one by one they began to ask him, "I'm not the one, am I, Lord?"

He replied, "One of you who is eating with me now will betray me. For I, the Son of Man, must die, as the Scriptures declared long ago. But how terrible it will be for my betrayer. Far better for him if he had never been born!"

Judas, the one who would betray him, also asked, "Teacher, I'm not the one, am I?"

And Jesus told him, "You have said it yourself."

As they were eating, Jesus took a loaf of bread and asked God's blessing on it. Then he broke it in pieces and gave it to the disciples, saying, "Take it and eat it, for this is my body." And he took a cup of wine and gave thanks to God for it. He gave it to them and said, "Each of you drink from it, for this is my blood, which seals the covenant between God and his people. It is poured out to forgive the sins of many. Mark my words—I will not drink wine again until the day I drink it new with you in my Father's Kingdom." (NLT)

Reading 14: Authority to Forgive

Mark 2:1-17

Several days later Jesus came back to Capernaum. The report went out that he was home. Many people had gathered. There was no room left, even in front of the door. Jesus was speaking {God's} word to them.

Four men came to him carrying a paralyzed man. Since they could not bring him to Jesus because of the crowd, they made an opening in the roof over the place where Jesus was. Then they lowered the cot on which the paralyzed man was lying.

When Jesus saw their faith, he said to the man, "Friend, your sins are forgiven."

Some scribes were sitting there. They thought, "Why does he talk this way? He's dishonoring God. Who besides God can forgive sins?"

At once, Jesus knew inwardly what they were thinking. He asked them, "Why do you have these thoughts? Is it easier to say to this paralyzed man, 'Your sins are forgiven,' or to say, 'Get up, pick up your cot, and walk'? I want you to know that the Son of Man has authority on earth to forgive sins." Then he said to the paralyzed man, "I'm telling you to get up, pick up your cot, and go home!"

The man got up, immediately picked up his cot, and walked away while everyone watched. Everyone was amazed and praised God, saying, "We have never seen anything like this."

Jesus went to the seashore again. Large crowds came to him, and he taught them.

When Jesus was leaving, he saw Levi, son of Alphaeus, sitting in a tax office. Jesus said to him, "Follow me!" So Levi got up and followed him.

Later Jesus was having dinner at Levi's house. Many tax collectors and sinners who were followers of Jesus were eating with him and his disciples. When the scribes who were Pharisees saw him eating with sinners and tax collectors, they asked his disciples, "Why does he eat with tax collectors and sinners?"

When Jesus heard that, he said to them, "Healthy people don't need a doctor; those who are sick do. I've come to call sinners, not people who think they have God's approval." (GWT)

Reading 15: Forgive and Be Forgiven

Luke 6:27-42

"But I say to you who hear, Love your enemies, do good to those who hate you, bless those who curse you, pray for those who abuse you. To one who strikes you on the cheek, offer the other also, and from one who takes away your cloak do not withhold your tunic either. Give to everyone who begs from you, and from one who takes away your goods do not demand them back. And as you wish that others would do to you, do so to them.

"If you love those who love you, what benefit is that to you? For even sinners love those who love them. And if you do good to those who do good to you, what benefit is that to you? For even sinners do the same. And if you lend to those from whom you expect to receive, what credit is that to you? Even sinners lend to sinners, to get back the same amount. But love your enemies, and do good, and lend, expecting nothing in return, and your reward will be great, and you will be sons of the Most High, for he is kind to the ungrateful and the evil. Be merciful, even as your Father is merciful. "Judge not, and you will not be judged; condemn not, and you will not be condemned; forgive, and you will be forgiven; give, and it will be given to you. Good measure, pressed down, shaken together, running over, will be put into your lap. For with the measure you use it will be measured back to you."

He also told them a parable: "Can a blind man lead a blind man? Will they not both fall into a pit? A disciple is not above his teacher, but everyone when he is fully trained will be like his teacher. Why do you see the speck that is in your brother's eye, but do not notice the log that is in your own eye? How can you say to your brother, 'Brother, let me take out the speck that is in your eye,' when you yourself do not see the log that is in your own eye? You hypocrite, first take the log out of your own eye, and then you will see clearly to take out the speck that is in your brother's eye. (ESV)

Reading 16: A Sinful Woman Forgiven

Luke 7:36-50

Now one of the Pharisees invited Jesus to have dinner with him, so he went to the Pharisee's house and reclined at the table. When a woman who had lived a sinful life in that town learned that Jesus was eating at the Pharisee's house, she brought an alabaster jar of perfume, and as she stood behind him at his feet weeping, she began to wet his feet with her tears. Then she wiped them with her hair, kissed them and poured perfume on them.

When the Pharisee who had invited him saw this, he said to himself, "If this man were a prophet, he would know who is touching him and what kind of woman she is--that she is a sinner."

Jesus answered him, "Simon, I have something to tell you."

"Tell me, teacher," he said.

"Two men owed money to a certain moneylender. One owed him five hundred denarii, and the other fifty. Neither of them had the money to pay him back, so he canceled the debts of both. Now which of them will love him more?"

Simon replied, "I suppose the one who had the bigger debt canceled."

"You have judged correctly," Jesus said.

Then he turned toward the woman and said to Simon, "Do you see this woman? I came into your house. You did not give me any water for my feet, but she wet my feet with her tears and wiped them with her hair. You did not give me a kiss, but this woman, from the time I entered, has not stopped kissing my feet. You did not put oil on my head, but she has poured perfume on my feet. Therefore, I tell you, her many sins have been forgiven--for she loved much. But he who has been forgiven little loves little."

Then Jesus said to her, "Your sins are forgiven."

The other guests began to say among themselves, "Who is this who even forgives sins?"

Jesus said to the woman, "Your faith has saved you; go in peace." (NIV)

Reading 17: If He Repents, Forgive Him

Luke 16:19-17:4

There was a rich man who was dressed in purple and fine linen and who feasted sumptuously every day. And at his gate lay a poor man named Lazarus, covered with sores, who longed to satisfy his hunger with what fell from the rich man's table; even the dogs would come and lick his sores. The poor man died and was carried away by the angels to be with Abraham. The rich man also died and was buried. In Hades, where he was being tormented, he looked up and saw Abraham far away with Lazarus by his side. He called out, 'Father Abraham, have mercy on me, and send Lazarus to dip the tip of his finger in water and cool my tongue; for I am in agony in these flames.' But Abraham said, 'Child, remember that during your lifetime you received your good things, and Lazarus in like manner evil things; but now he is comforted here, and you are in agony. Besides all this, between you and us a great chasm has been fixed, so that those who might want to pass from here to you cannot do so, and no one can cross from there to us.' He said, 'Then, father, I beg you to send him to my father's house-- for I have five brothers--that he may warn them, so that they will not also come into this place of torment.' Abraham replied, 'They have Moses and the prophets; they should listen to them.' He said, 'No, father Abraham; but if someone goes to them from the dead, they will repent.' He said to him, 'If they do not listen to

Moses and the prophets, neither will they be convinced even if someone rises from the dead.' "

Jesus said to his disciples, "Occasions for stumbling are bound to come, but woe to anyone by whom they come! It would be better for you if a millstone were hung around your neck and you were thrown into the sea than for you to cause one of these little ones to stumble. Be on your guard! If another disciple sins, you must rebuke the offender, and if there is repentance, you must forgive. And if the same person sins against you seven times a day, and turns back to you seven times and says, 'I repent,' you must forgive." (NRSV)

Reading 18: Father Forgive Them

Luke 23:26-43

As they led Jesus away, Simon of Cyrene, who was coming in from the country just then, was forced to follow Jesus and carry his cross. Great crowds trailed along behind, including many grief-stricken women. But Jesus turned and said to them, "Daughters of Jerusalem, don't weep for me, but weep for yourselves and for your children. For the days are coming when they will say, 'Fortunate indeed are the women who are childless, the wombs that have not borne a child and the breasts that have never nursed.' People will beg the mountains to fall on them and the hills to bury them. For if these things are done when the tree is green, what will happen when it is dry?"

Two others, both criminals, were led out to be executed with him. Finally, they came to a place called The Skull. All three were crucified there—Jesus on the center cross, and the two criminals on either side.

Jesus said, "Father, forgive these people, because they don't know what they are doing." And the soldiers gambled for his clothes by throwing dice.

The crowd watched, and the leaders laughed and scoffed. "He saved others," they said, "let him save himself if he is really God's Chosen One, the Messiah." The soldiers mocked him, too, by offering him a drink of sour wine. They called out to him, "If you are the King of the Jews, save yourself!" A signboard was nailed to the cross above him with these words: "This is the King of the Jews."

One of the criminals hanging beside him scoffed, "So you're the Messiah, are you? Prove it by saving yourself—and us, too, while you're at it!"

But the other criminal protested, "Don't you fear God even when you are dying? We deserve to die for our evil deeds, but this man hasn't done anything wrong." Then he said, "Jesus, remember me when you come into your Kingdom."

And Jesus replied, "I assure you, today you will be with me in paradise."

(NLT)

Reading 19: Neither Do I Condemn You

John 7:53-8:11

Jesus went to the Mount of Olives. Early the next morning he returned to the temple courtyard. All the people went to him, so he sat down and began to teach them.

The scribes and the Pharisees brought a woman who had been caught committing adultery. They made her stand in front of everyone and asked Jesus, "Teacher, we caught this woman in the act of adultery. In his teachings, Moses ordered us to stone women like this to death. What do you say?" They asked this to test him. They wanted to find a reason to bring charges against him.

Jesus bent down and used his finger to write on the ground. When they persisted in asking him questions, he straightened up and said, "The person who is sinless should be the first to throw a stone at her." Then he bent down again and continued writing on the ground.

One by one, beginning with the older men, the scribes and Pharisees left. Jesus was left alone with the woman. Then Jesus straightened up and asked her, "Where did they go? Has anyone condemned you?"

The woman answered, "No one, sir."

Jesus said, "I don't condemn you either. Go! From now on don't sin."

(GWT)

Reading 20: That They May Receive Forgiveness

Acts 26:1-23

So Agrippa said to Paul, "You have permission to speak for yourself." Then Paul stretched out his hand and made his defense:

"I consider myself fortunate that it is before you, King Agrippa, I am going to make my defense today against all the accusations of the Jews, especially because you are familiar with all the customs and controversies of the Jews. Therefore I beg you to listen to me patiently.

"My manner of life from my youth, spent from the beginning among my own nation and in Jerusalem, is known by all the Jews. They have known for a long time, if they are willing to testify, that according to the strictest party of our religion I have lived as a Pharisee. And now I stand here on trial because of my hope in the promise made by God to our fathers, to which our twelve tribes hope to attain, as they earnestly worship night and day. And for this hope I am accused by Jews, O king! Why is it thought incredible by any of you that God raises the dead?

"I myself was convinced that I ought to do many things in opposing the name of Jesus of Nazareth. And I did so in Jerusalem. I not only locked up many of the saints in prison after receiving authority from the chief priests, but when they were put to death I cast my vote against them. And I punished them often in all the synagogues and tried to make them blaspheme, and in raging fury against them I persecuted them even to foreign cities.

"In this connection I journeyed to Damascus with the authority and commission of the chief priests. At midday, O king, I saw on the way a light from heaven, brighter than the sun, that shone around me and those who journeyed with me. And when we had all fallen to the ground, I heard a voice saying to me in the Hebrew language, 'Saul, Saul, why are you persecuting me? It is hard for you to kick against the goads.' And I said, 'Who are you, Lord?' And the Lord said, 'I am Jesus whom you are persecuting. But rise and stand upon your feet, for I have appeared to you for this purpose, to appoint you as a servant and witness to the things in which you have seen me and to those in which I will appear to you, delivering you from your people and from the Gentiles— to whom I am sending you

to open their eyes, so that they may turn from darkness to light and from the power of Satan to God, that they may receive forgiveness of sins and a place among those who are sanctified by faith in me.'

"Therefore, O King Agrippa, I was not disobedient to the heavenly vision, but declared first to those in Damascus, then in Jerusalem and throughout all the region of Judea, and also to the Gentiles, that they should repent and turn to God, performing deeds in keeping with their repentance. For this reason the Jews seized me in the temple and tried to kill me. To this day I have had the help that comes from God, and so I stand here testifying both to small and great, saying nothing but what the prophets and Moses said would come to pass: that the Christ must suffer and that, by being the first to rise from the dead, he would proclaim light both to our people and to the Gentiles." (ESV)

Reading 21: Peace With God, Eternal Life

Romans 5:1-20

Therefore, since we have been justified through faith, we have peace with God through our Lord Jesus Christ, through whom we have gained access by faith into this grace in which we now stand. And we rejoice in the hope of the glory of God. Not only so, but we also rejoice in our sufferings, because we know that suffering produces perseverance; perseverance, character; and character, hope. And hope does not disappoint us, because God has poured out his love into our hearts by the Holy Spirit, whom he has given us.

You see, at just the right time, when we were still powerless, Christ died for the ungodly. Very rarely will anyone die for a righteous man, though for a good man someone might possibly dare to die. But God demonstrates his own love for us in this: While we were still sinners, Christ died for us.

Since we have now been justified by his blood, how much more shall we be saved from God's wrath through him! For if, when we were God's enemies, we were reconciled to him through the death of his Son, how much more, having been reconciled, shall we be saved through his life! Not only is this so, but we also rejoice in God through our Lord Jesus Christ, through whom we have now received reconciliation.

Therefore, just as sin entered the world through one man, and death through sin, and in this way death came to all men, because all sinned-- for before the law was given, sin was in the world. But sin is not taken into account when there is no law. Nevertheless, death reigned from the time of Adam to the time of Moses, even over those who did not sin by breaking a command, as did Adam, who was a pattern of the one to come.

But the gift is not like the trespass. For if the many died by the trespass of the one man, how much more did God's grace and the gift that came by the grace of the one man, Jesus Christ, overflow to the many! Again, the gift of God is not like the result of the one man's sin: The judgment followed one sin and brought condemnation, but the gift followed many trespasses and brought justification. For if, by the trespass of the one man, death reigned through that one man, how much more will those who receive God's abundant provision of grace and of the gift of righteousness reign in life through the one man, Jesus Christ.

Consequently, just as the result of one trespass was condemnation for all men, so also the result of one act of righteousness was justification that brings life for all men. For just as through the disobedience of the one man the many were made sinners, so also through the obedience of the one man the many will be made righteous.

The law was added so that the trespass might increase. But where sin increased, grace increased all the more, (NIV)

Reading 22: Forgive and Comfort

II Corinthians 2:1-11

So I made up my mind not to make you another painful visit. For if I cause you pain, who is there to make me glad but the one whom I have pained? And I wrote as I did, so that when I came, I might not suffer pain from those who should have made me rejoice; for I am confident about all of you, that my joy would be the joy of all of you. For I wrote you out of much distress and anguish of heart and with many tears, not to cause you pain, but to let you know the abundant love that I have for you.

But if anyone has caused pain, he has caused it not to me, but to some extent--not to exaggerate it--to all of you. This punishment by the majority is enough for such a person; so now instead you should forgive and console him, so that he may not be overwhelmed by excessive sorrow. So I urge you to reaffirm your love for him. I wrote for this reason: to test you and to know whether you are obedient in everything. Anyone whom you forgive, I also forgive. What I have forgiven, if I have forgiven anything, has been for your sake in the presence of Christ. And we do this so that we may not be outwitted by Satan; for we are not ignorant of his designs. (NRSV)

Reading 23: Alive Together With Christ

Ephesians 1:3-2:10

How we praise God, the Father of our Lord Jesus Christ, who has blessed us with every spiritual blessing in the heavenly realms because we belong to Christ. Long ago, even before he made the world, God loved us and chose us in Christ to be holy and without fault in his eyes. His unchanging plan has always been to adopt us into his own family by bringing us to himself through Jesus Christ. And this gave him great pleasure.

So we praise God for the wonderful kindness he has poured out on us because we belong to his dearly loved Son. He is so rich in kindness that he purchased our freedom through the blood of his Son, and our sins are forgiven. He has showered his kindness on us, along with all wisdom and understanding.

God's secret plan has now been revealed to us; it is a plan centered on Christ, designed long ago according to his good pleasure. And this is his plan: At the right time he will bring everything together under the authority of Christ—everything in heaven and on earth. Furthermore, because of Christ, we have received an inheritance from God, for he chose us from the beginning, and all things happen just as he decided long ago. God's purpose was that we who were the first to trust in Christ should praise our glorious God. And now you also have heard the truth, the Good News that God saves you. And when you believed in Christ, he identified you as his own by giving you the

Holy Spirit, whom he promised long ago. The Spirit is God's guarantee that he will give us everything he promised and that he has purchased us to be his own people. This is just one more reason for us to praise our glorious God.

Ever since I first heard of your strong faith in the Lord Jesus and your love for Christians everywhere, I have never stopped thanking God for you. I pray for you constantly, asking God, the glorious Father of our Lord Jesus Christ, to give you spiritual wisdom and understanding, so that you might grow in your knowledge of God. I pray that your hearts will be flooded with light so that you can understand the wonderful future he has promised to those he called. I want you to realize what a rich and glorious inheritance he has given to his people.

I pray that you will begin to understand the incredible greatness of his power for us who believe him. This is the same mighty power that raised Christ from the dead and seated him in the place of honor at God's right hand in the heavenly realms. Now he is far above any ruler or authority or power or leader or anything else in this world or in the world to come. And God has put all things under the authority of Christ, and he gave him this authority for the benefit of the church. And the church is his body; it is filled by Christ, who fills everything everywhere with his presence.

Once you were dead, doomed forever because of your many sins. You used to live just like the rest of the world, full of sin, obeying Satan, the mighty prince of the power of the air. He is the spirit at work in the hearts of those who refuse to obey God. All of us used to live that way, following the passions and desires of our evil nature. We were born with an evil nature, and we were under God's anger just like everyone else.

But God is so rich in mercy, and he loved us so very much, that even while we were dead because of our sins, he gave us life when he raised Christ from the dead. (It is only by God's special favor that you have been saved!) For he raised us from the dead along with Christ, and we are seated with him in the heavenly realms—all because we are one with Christ Jesus. And so God can always point to us as examples of the incredible wealth of his favor and kindness toward us, as shown in all he has done for us through Christ Jesus.

God saved you by his special favor when you believed. And you can't take credit for this; it is a gift from God. Salvation is not a reward for the good things we have done, so none of us can boast about it. For we are God's masterpiece. He has created us anew in Christ Jesus, so that we can do the good things he planned for us long ago.

(NLT)

Reading 24: Forgiving One Another

Ephesians 4:17-32

So I tell you and encourage you in the Lord's name not to live any longer like other people in the world. Their minds are set on worthless things. They can't understand because they are in the dark. They are excluded from the life that God approves of because of their ignorance and stubbornness. Since they no longer have any sense of shame, they have become promiscuous. They practice every kind of sexual perversion with a constant desire for more.

But that is not what you learned from Christ's teachings. You have certainly heard his message and have been taught his ways. The truth is in Jesus. You were taught to change the way you were living. The person you used to be will ruin you through desires that deceive you. However, you were taught to have a new attitude. You were also taught to become a new person created to be like God, truly righteous and holy.

So then, get rid of lies. Speak the truth to each other, because we are all members of the same body.

Be angry without sinning. Don't go to bed angry. Don't give the devil any opportunity {to work}.

Thieves must quit stealing and, instead, they must work hard. They should do something good with their hands so that they'll have something to share with those in need.

Don't say anything that would hurt {another person}. Instead, speak only what is good so that you can give help wherever it is needed. That way, what you say will help those who hear you. Don't give God's Holy Spirit any reason to be upset with you. He has put his seal on you for the day you will be set free {from the world of sin}.

Get rid of your bitterness, hot tempers, anger, loud quarreling, cursing, and hatred. Be kind to each other, sympathetic, forgiving each other as God has forgiven you through Christ. (GWT)

Reading 25: Reconciled By His Death

Colossians 1:3-23

We always thank God, the Father of our Lord Jesus Christ, when we pray for you, since we heard of your faith in Christ Jesus and of the love that you have for all the saints, because of the hope laid up for you in heaven. Of this you have heard before in the word of the truth, the gospel, which has come to you, as indeed in the whole world it is bearing fruit and growing—as it also does among you, since the day you heard it and understood the grace of God in truth, just as you learned it from Epaphras our beloved fellow servant. He is a faithful minister of Christ on your behalf and has made known to us your love in the Spirit.

And so, from the day we heard, we have not ceased to pray for you, asking that you may be filled with the knowledge of his will in all spiritual wisdom and understanding, so as to walk in a manner worthy of the Lord, fully pleasing to him, bearing fruit in every good work and increasing in the knowledge of God. May you be strengthened with all power, according to his glorious might, for all endurance and patience with joy, giving thanks to the Father, who has qualified you to share in the inheritance of the saints in light. He has delivered us from the domain of darkness and transferred us to the kingdom of his beloved Son, in whom we have redemption, the forgiveness of sins.

He is the image of the invisible God, the firstborn of all creation. For by him all things were created, in heaven and on earth, visible and invisible, whether thrones or dominions or rulers or authorities—all things were created through him and for him. And he is before all things, and in him all things hold together. And he is the head of the body, the church. He is the beginning, the firstborn from the dead, that in everything he might be preeminent. For in him all the fullness of God was pleased to dwell, and through him to reconcile to himself all things, whether on earth or in heaven, making peace by the blood of his cross.

And you, who once were alienated and hostile in mind, doing evil deeds, he has now reconciled in his body of flesh by his death, in order to present you holy and blameless and above reproach before him, if indeed you continue in the faith, stable and steadfast, not shifting from the hope of the gospel that you heard, which has been proclaimed in all creation under heaven, and of which I, Paul, became a minister. (ESV)

Reading 26: As The Lord Forgave You

Colossians 3:1-17

Since, then, you have been raised with Christ, set your hearts on things above, where Christ is seated at the right hand of God. Set your minds on things above, not on earthly things. For you died, and your life is now hidden with Christ in God. When Christ, who is your life, appears, then you also will appear with him in glory.

Put to death, therefore, whatever belongs to your earthly nature: sexual immorality, impurity, lust, evil desires and greed, which is idolatry. Because of these, the wrath of God is coming. You used to walk in these ways, in the life you once lived. But now you must rid yourselves of all such things as these: anger, rage, malice, slander, and filthy language from your lips. Do not lie to each other, since you have taken off your old self with its practices and have put on the new self, which is being renewed in knowledge in the image of its Creator. Here there is no Greek or Jew, circumcised or uncircumcised, barbarian, Scythian, slave or free, but Christ is all, and is in all.

Therefore, as God's chosen people, holy and dearly loved, clothe yourselves with compassion, kindness, humility, gentleness and patience. Bear with each other and forgive whatever grievances you may have against one another. Forgive as the Lord forgave you. And over all these virtues put on love, which binds them all together in perfect unity.

Let the peace of Christ rule in your hearts, since as members of one body you were called to peace. And be thankful. Let the word of

Christ dwell in you richly as you teach and admonish one another with all wisdom, and as you sing psalms, hymns and spiritual songs with gratitude in your hearts to God. And whatever you do, whether in word or deed, do it all in the name of the Lord Jesus, giving thanks to God the Father through him. (NIV)

Reading 27: Mediator of a New Covenant

Hebrews 9:11-10:10

But when Christ came as a high priest of the good things that have come, then through the greater and perfect tent (not made with hands, that is, not of this creation), he entered once for all into the Holy Place, not with the blood of goats and calves, but with his own blood, thus obtaining eternal redemption. For if the blood of goats and bulls, with the sprinkling of the ashes of a heifer, sanctifies those who have been defiled so that their flesh is purified, how much more will the blood of Christ, who through the eternal Spirit offered himself without blemish to God, purify our conscience from dead works to worship the living God!

For this reason he is the mediator of a new covenant, so that those who are called may receive the promised eternal inheritance, because a death has occurred that redeems them from the transgressions under the first covenant. Where a will is involved, the death of the one who made it must be established. For a will takes effect only at death, since it is not in force as long as the one who made it is alive. Hence not even the first covenant was inaugurated without blood. For when every commandment had been told to all the people by Moses in accordance with the law, he took the blood of calves and goats, with water and scarlet wool and hyssop, and sprinkled both the scroll itself and all the people, saying, "This is the blood of the covenant that God has ordained for you." And in the same way he sprinkled with the blood both the tent and all the vessels used in worship. Indeed, under the law almost everything is purified with blood, and without the shedding of blood there is no forgiveness of sins.

Thus it was necessary for the sketches of the heavenly things to be purified with these rites, but the heavenly things themselves need better sacrifices than these. For Christ did not enter a sanctuary made by human hands, a mere copy of the true one, but he entered into heaven itself, now to appear in the presence of God on our behalf. Nor was it to offer himself again and again, as the high priest enters the Holy Place year after year with blood that is not his own; for then he would have had to suffer again and again since the foundation of the world. But as it is, he has appeared once for all at the end of the age to remove sin by the sacrifice of himself. And just as it is appointed for mortals to die once, and after that the judgment, so Christ, having been offered once to bear the sins of many, will appear a second time, not to deal with sin, but to save those who are eagerly waiting for him.

Since the law has only a shadow of the good things to come and not the true form of these realities, it can never, by the same sacrifices that are continually offered year after year, make perfect those who approach. Otherwise, would they not have ceased being offered, since the worshipers, cleansed once for all, would no longer have any consciousness of sin? But in these sacrifices there is a reminder of sin year after year. For it is impossible for the blood of bulls and goats to take away sins. Consequently, when Christ came into the world, he said,

"Sacrifices and offerings you have not desired,
but a body you have prepared for me;
in burnt offerings and sin offerings
you have taken no pleasure.
Then I said, 'See, God, I have come to do your will, O God'

(in the scroll of the book it is written of me)."

When he said above, "You have neither desired nor taken pleasure in sacrifices and offerings and burnt offerings and sin offerings" (these are offered according to the law), then he added, "See, I have come to do your will." He abolishes the first in order to establish the second. And it is by God's will that we have been sanctified through the offering of the body of Jesus Christ once for all. (NRSV)

Reading 28: Our Great High Priest

Hebrews 10:11-39

Under the old covenant, the priest stands before the altar day after day, offering sacrifices that can never take away sins. But our High Priest offered himself to God as one sacrifice for sins, good for all time. Then he sat down at the place of highest honor at God's right hand. There he waits until his enemies are humbled as a footstool under his feet. For by that one offering he perfected forever all those whom he is making holy.

And the Holy Spirit also testifies that this is so. First he says,

"This is the new covenant I will make
 with my people on that day, says the Lord:
I will put my laws in their hearts
 so they will understand them,
and I will write them on their minds
 so they will obey them."

Then he adds,

"I will never again remember
 their sins and lawless deeds."

Now when sins have been forgiven, there is no need to offer any more sacrifices.

And so, dear brothers and sisters, we can boldly enter heaven's Most Holy Place because of the blood of Jesus. This is the new, life-giving way that Christ has opened up for us through the sacred curtain, by means of his death for us.

And since we have a great High Priest who rules over God's people, let us go right into the presence of God, with true hearts fully trusting him. For our evil consciences have been sprinkled with Christ's blood to make us clean, and our bodies have been washed with pure water.

Without wavering, let us hold tightly to the hope we say we have, for God can be trusted to keep his promise. Think of ways to encourage one another to outbursts of love and good deeds. And let us not neglect our meeting together, as some people do, but encourage and warn each other, especially now that the day of his coming back again is drawing near.

Dear friends, if we deliberately continue sinning after we have received a full knowledge of the truth, there is no other sacrifice that will cover these sins. There will be nothing to look forward to but the terrible expectation of God's judgment and the raging fire that will consume his enemies. Anyone who refused to obey the law of Moses was put to death without mercy on the testimony of two or three witnesses. Think how much more terrible the punishment will be for those who have trampled on the Son of God and have treated the blood of the covenant as if it were common and unholy. Such people have insulted and enraged the Holy Spirit who brings God's mercy to his people.

For we know the one who said,

"I will take vengeance.
 I will repay those who deserve it."

He also said,

"The Lord will judge his own people."

It is a terrible thing to fall into the hands of the living God.

Don't ever forget those early days when you first learned about Christ. Remember how you remained faithful even though it meant terrible suffering. Sometimes you were exposed to public ridicule and were beaten, and sometimes you helped others who were suffering the same things. You suffered along with those who were thrown into jail. When all you owned was taken from you, you accepted it with joy. You knew you had better things waiting for you in eternity.

Do not throw away this confident trust in the Lord, no matter what happens. Remember the great reward it brings you! Patient endurance is what you need now, so you will continue to do God's will. Then you will receive all that he has promised.

"For in just a little while,
 the Coming One will come and not delay.
 And a righteous person will live by faith.
 But I will have no pleasure in anyone who turns away."

But we are not like those who turn their backs on God and seal their fate. We have faith that assures our salvation. (NLT)

Reading 29: Patience and Prayer

James 5:7-20

Brothers and sisters, be patient until the Lord comes again. See how farmers wait for their precious crops to grow. They wait patiently for fall and spring rains. You, too, must be patient. Don't give up hope. The Lord will soon be here. Brothers and sisters, stop complaining about each other, or you will be condemned. Realize that the judge is standing at the door.

Brothers and sisters, follow the example of the prophets who spoke in the name of the Lord. They were patient when they suffered unjustly. We consider those who endure to be blessed. You have heard about Job's endurance. You saw that the Lord ended Job's suffering because the Lord is compassionate and merciful.

Above all things, my brothers and sisters, do not take an oath on anything in heaven or on earth. Do not take any oath. If you mean yes, say yes. If you mean no, say no. Do this so that you won't be condemned.

If any of you are having trouble, pray. If you are happy, sing psalms. If you are sick, call for the church leaders. Have them pray for you and anoint you with olive oil in the name of the Lord. (Prayers offered in faith will save those who are sick, and the Lord will cure them.) If you have sinned, you will be forgiven. So admit your sins to each other, and pray for each other so that you will be healed.

Prayers offered by those who have God's approval are effective. Elijah was human like us. Yet, when he prayed that it wouldn't rain, no rain fell on the ground for three-and-a-half years. Then he prayed again. It rained, and the ground produced crops.

My brothers and sisters, if one of you wanders from the truth, someone can bring that person back. Realize that whoever brings a sinner back from the error of his ways will save him from death, and many sins will be forgiven. (GWT)

Reading 30: Confess Your Sins

I John 1:5-2:6

This is the message we have heard from him and proclaim to you, that God is light, and in him is no darkness at all. If we say we have fellowship with him while we walk in darkness, we lie and do not practice the truth. But if we walk in the light, as he is in the light, we have fellowship with one another, and the blood of Jesus his Son cleanses us from all sin. If we say we have no sin, we deceive ourselves, and the truth is not in us. If we confess our sins, he is faithful and just to forgive us our sins and to cleanse us from all unrighteousness. If we say we have not sinned, we make him a liar, and his word is not in us.

My little children, I am writing these things to you so that you may not sin. But if anyone does sin, we have an advocate with the Father, Jesus Christ the righteous. He is the propitiation for our sins, and not for ours only but also for the sins of the whole world. And by this we know that we have come to know him, if we keep his commandments. Whoever says "I know him" but does not keep his commandments is a liar, and the truth is not in him, but whoever keeps his word, in him truly the love of God is perfected. By this we may be sure that we are in him: whoever says he abides in him ought to walk in the same way in which he walked. (ESV) eBooks by TheBiblePeople.com

Parables of Jesus: The Stories of Christ Arranged by Topic
365 Encouraging Bible Verses
The Book of Proverbs arranged by Topic

Year Long Bible Reading Series
Jesus: 45 Scripture Readings that Overview His Life
30 Scripture Readings on Great Women of the Bible
30 Scripture Readings on Great Men of the Bible
30 Scripture Readings on Getting to Know God
30 Scripture Readings on Easter
30 Scripture Readings on Finding Strength
30 Scripture Readings for Spiritual Growth
30 Scripture Readings on God's Amazing Power
30 Scripture Reading on Praising God

Visit TheBiblePeople.com to learn more about these books

www.ingramcontent.com/pod-product-compliance
Lightning Source LLC
Chambersburg PA
CBHW071329040426
42444CB00009B/2113